RYA Intermediate Windsurfing

Words by Simon Bornhoft
Technical editor Amanda Van Santen

© RYA Simon Bornhoft
First Published 2008
The Royal Yachting Association
RYA House, Ensign Way, Hamble
Southampton SO31 4YA
Tel: 0845 345 0400
Fax: 0845 345 0329
Email: publications@rya.org.uk
Web: www.rya.org.uk
ISBN: 978-1-o905104-58-1
RYA Order Code: G51

A CIP record of this book is available from the British Library

Note: While all reasonable care has been taken in the preparation of this book, the publisher takes no responsibility for the use of the methods or products or contracts described in the book.

Telephone 0845 345 0400 for a free copy of our Publications Catalogue.

Cover Design: Pete Galvin
Photographs: Karen Bornhoft and Mark Warner Abu Soma
Illustrations: Pete Galvin
Typeset: Creativebyte
Proofreading and indexing: Alan Thatcher
Printed in China through: World Print
Acknowlegments: Mark Warner, Tushingham and Gul, Simon Winkley.

Totally Chlorine Free   Sustainable Forests

Contents

Chapter		Page

RYA Intermediate Windsurfing Course

No matter what level of windsurfer, we all stand on a board with hands and feet roughly shoulder width apart as we cruise along. From this position, we aim to control the equipment and conditions in order to enjoy the great thrill of windsurfing. Look at a very experienced windsurfer blasting along, they aren't actually doing anything wildly different than those with less experience. What they are demonstrating, however, is their ability to identify, use and commit to a small number of simple, yet very specific, techniques. Success in windsurfing, therefore, is made possible by the understanding and practice of the core skills.

To help make your progression as quick and easy as possible, the RYA and Simon Bornhoft have created the Fastfwd Formula. This has been specifically designed to enable windsurfers to master the exact skills that truly work – not just at one particular time in the learning curve – but right through the sport into the most advanced levels. So, from here on, rather than having to re-learn new skills you will, with a little time and effort, progress quicker and more effectively as you gain a deeper and more fluid understanding of the basics.

Upon completing the intermediate course or specific clinics, the instructor will log your progression in the RYA National Windsurfing Logbook and Syllabus (G47). The centre principal or chief instructor will decide whether a certificate is to be awarded or advise you that further practice is required providing you with a clear pathway to gain your certificate.

Fastfwd Coaching within National Windsurfing Scheme:
- Identifies the most influential skills in windsurfing.
- Simplifies and constantly develops these vital and re-usable skills.
- Every skill is transferable into all levels of the sport.

Using the *fastfwd* Formula

The Formula has five principle elements, each of which has a very specific purpose. Whilst you might, on occasions, heavily accentuate one particular element, they all actually link together and support your actions and aspirations on a board. The Formula always starts with Vision, and works in a continuous circle, creating a systematic reminder, guide and self-diagnosis system.

You'll see how the whole Formula forms the basis of virtually everything you'll do on ANY board - Getting Going, Steering, Early Planing, Harnessing, Footstraps and Blasting Control.

Transition skills

When it comes to transitions, principally tacking and gybing, we still rely on elements from the Formula, but we also require two very specific skills - 'Shifting and Switching' and the 'Rig Rotator' to help us round the corners!

'Shifting & Switching' - A well-timed movement of the hips and feet mid turn.

'Rig Rotator' – A specific movement to 'rotate' the rig in non-planing & planing gybes (also used in helicopter tacks and more advanced moves too).

Using This Book

The aim of this book is to assist you through the earlier stages of the sport highlighting *the* defining skills and objectives that encourage quick progression. We will start off by looking at the relevance of each element in the Formula and then move onto the common topics that you're likely to encounter and see how to master. When you're on the water, it's so often the smallest basic point that can be the defining action that suddenly brings everything together. So don't overlook the basic points, accentuate them! To give you some added assistance we've also included some **Top Tips** to focus on and a coach's corner. These might reiterate certain points *again*, or add subtle detail to help make the difference. They should all contribute towards your progress.

Finally, you may sometimes hear the phrase 'windsurfing is easy'! Well, if it was that easy we'd all be world champion after our first season. In truth, like most sports, windsurfing is the epitome of the 'effort equals reward' equation. Just being told what to do isn't enough, you need to be prepared to practise, develop skills, make mistakes and just keep at it. Anyone can become a very accomplished windsurfer.

Here's a short list of considerations that, when combined with focusing on the correct technique, will go a long way to enhance your improvement.

- Always try to accentuate your actions – for example you might feel you're bending your knees or leaning outboard, but are you really?
- Try not to overlook the simple points – going back to basics usually works – that's what the Formula is for!
- If things 'go wrong' – look at what you were doing just before you fell in, or dropped the rig, and work through the Formula to help diagnose the problem.
- Accentuate one element at a time – multi tasking is not easy at speed.
- There will be times for exertion, but if it's a constant struggle, stop… think, get some advice and a clear purpose and have another go.
- Whilst the desire for planing windsurfing is understandable, remember to use lighter winds to practise the finer details.

Finally, enjoy your time on the water, learn from the experience of our RYA Instructors, others on the water and feel proud to be a part of this wonderful sport!

VISION Helps Maintain Your Sailing Line

Looking where you want to go has a truly incredible effect on technique in every aspect of windsurfing. So it's no surprise that VISION sits right at the top of the formula. It is such a simple point that many people don't quite believe its value.

With VISION it is simply a case of no matter what else you might be doing, look where you want to go and not at the kit. This has an incredible effect on your balance, stability, direction and confidence. It can also contribute towards making your actions more fluid and dynamic.

Top Tips

- So simple, but so important – Look where you want to go.
- Look forward for – early planing, harnessing, footstraps, improving stance, reading the wind/water state and noticing changes in your sailing line.
- Look downwind – to sail or turn downwind, for example; when increasing speed or looking through a gybe.
- Look upwind – to sail or turn upwind, when controlling excess speed or preparing to tack.
- For transitions and manoeuvres – look where you want to go especially for the entry and exit of the move.

Techniques

You will see how VISION is constantly reinforced throughout this book, but here are some defining examples of when VISION really helps.

Getting Going & Blasting

Chin up and looking forward establishes a good stance, calmer composure and a positive sailing line. When harnessing & finding foot straps look forward before and after hooking in, or when going for the straps.

Gybing

Looking into the gybe on entry and out of the gybe on exit improves rig control, timing of rig release, and leads you through the gybe.

Upwind

Turning the head over the front shoulder helps you to spot gusts and lulls and takes you upwind.

Coach's Corner

Try a few runs, tacks or gybes where you 'just' focus on looking forward and where you want to go.

Tacking

Looking upwind on entry and then out of the tack on exit is instrumental for tidy, well executed tacks.

Losing Your Head

'Gear gazing' immediately decreases your chances of success, especially when exiting moves or going for the harness or straps.

TRIM Keeps the Board Flat

The simple principle of the board's TRIM should be like the foundations of a house, flat and stable. From cruising around in marginal or comfortable planing conditions to fast blasting over white capped seas, your board, no matter what size or shape, should be kept flat. You'll see that the position on the board, your Stance and ability to oppose the rig's force, position and movement (see Balance section page 11) link back into reinforcing this simple principle. If the board isn't trimmed flat, problems immediately occur. Trim, therefore, is a constant priority for getting going, harnessing, footstraps and blasting control.

For this section, we're going to concentrate on how to position and direct the forces through your feet.

Trim in the footstraps

To encourage acceleration – push through the toes.

To control acceleration – dig and weight the heels, pulling up on toes to lock the windward rail down.

Trim out of the footstraps

Front foot points forward – to drive the board forward and keep it flat front to back.

Rear foot goes across the board - to keep it flat across its width, controlling sideways tilt.

Slower speeds – feet move forward and inboard, with increase of toe pressure.

Higher speeds – feet move back and outboard, with increase of heel pressure.

Using TRIM for Getting Going & Early Planing

Although you may not yet have experienced all of the following scenarios, it is important to grasp how a good understanding of TRIM is an integral part of your progression through the sport. You will also find that TRIM is a major factor in achieving comfortable blasting control.

When going for the footstraps, always make sure that the foot is next to the strap, avoiding big movements that could upset the board TRIM.

Slow to plane?

Bringing both feet forward and pushing through the toes prevents the tail from dragging and helps acceleration.

The feet are often placed further forward than you think, even in front of the front straps.

As the board accelerates, move the feet towards the windward rail and back, weighting the heels to control acceleration.

Marginal Blasting
Losing Speed?

In marginal winds, try to push through the toes (especially the front foot) to drive the board flat. This is best achieved if you lift and lock the hips to form a Straight 7 (see page 17) stance, to keep the rig upright.

> **Top Tip**
> - In difficult situations you will find bending the back leg helps maintain TRIM.

Strong Wind Blasting
Losing Control?

To control an excessively speeding or railing board (when the windward rail of the board lifts out of the water uncontrolled), pull up on the toes, especially in the front strap. This links into our Super 7 drop and dig stance which weights the heels to prevent the windward rail from lifting. (see page 19).

If you are heading too much upwind, you may be sheeted out too far with the rig or flexing the front leg too much.

Sinking

It's very common to overweight the back foot, which causes the tail to sink, prevents acceleration and often reduces control. This is less apparent on larger volume boards (170L+), but it can be a real problem in marginal conditions or on lower volume boards.

BALANCE Forms Your Framework

It is often said that windsurfing is all about BALANCE and anyone who has lost their balance and fallen off a board will probably agree with this statement. But actually it's not all about their BALANCE, it's more the ability to constantly *oppose* and counterbalance the rig's position, forces and movement that makes a better windsurfer.

In windsurfing everything revolves around the simple principle. We constantly need to maintain and accentuate a counterbalance for getting going, early planing, harnessing, steering and blasting control. You will see in this next section how BALANCE is an integral part of improving Trim, Power & Stance. It is also a fundamental action when securing yourself in the footstraps and the absolute foundation of staying on the board during tacks, gybes and every other transition.

For example, when steering downwind, getting going or finding the front strap, the rig is leant forward as the body leans or moves back to Counterbalance. The same principle is applied when steering upwind or going for the back strap; the rig is leant back as the body leans forward *to counterbalance*.

Rig forward, body back – Always oppose the rig's pull, force and movement to create a Counterbalance.

Oppose the rig – In most instances maintain a good distance from the rig by extending the front arm.

Upwind & Lulls, Rig back, body forward – When heading upwind, or if the wind lulls, rake the rig back and lean the body forward. It feels as if the clew is being pushed towards the tail as the shoulders lean forward and to windward.

Using Balance for Tacking and Gybing

Continually opposing the rig's position, forces and movement in transitions, helps maintain your counterbalance and encourages the turning motion. In the tacking section you will discover this same opposing theme.

Tacking

Entry The rig is raked back, so the feet, hips and front hand move forward.

Mid tack The mast is pushed *across* to leeward and the body opposes this movement by shifting to windward.

Exit Only then is the mast drawn forward as the body sinks back towards the tail.

Gybing

Gybing is probably the greatest test of counterbalance skills, you need to constantly TRIM and adjust the rig's position as the board turns. The following basic principles apply whether it's your first ever gybe or high speed carving turn. See the gybing chapter (page 60), for more information.

> ### Losing to the opposition
> 9/10, when something goes wrong it is usually due to a lack of counterbalance. This could be due to pulling the mast too close to the body or your body leaning the same way as the rig.

POWER Channels the Rig's Forces

POWER is acheived by the simple action of sheeting in (pulling the boom in, back and down).

It is easy to see the importance of sheeting the sail in to generate speed, however the action of also pulling down on the boom, puts pressure through the mast base, which helps TRIM and also stabilises the rig and body. It's an integral part of getting going, early planing, harnessing, finding footstraps and especially maintaining comfort and control at speed.

Techniques

Because the technique is understated and often overlooked, it's worth highlighting how often it's used throughout the sport, even if you're not windsurfing at faster speeds yet. Throughout this book, we often refer to power to make sure the rig is always being used to drive the board forwards.

To improve your ability to sheet the rig in – make sure the front arm is extended, with both hands (and the harness lines) further down the boom, to get more leverage over the clew.

Whether you are in or out of the harness – always avoid having the rig sheeted too far out.

In marginal winds – or just prior to using the harness, body weight is used to sheet the boom in, back and down.

To accentuate Power – use your whole body weight to hang down off the boom by sitting down hard in the harness.

In stronger winds – it is imperative to put all your effort into keeping weight down through the harness line and maintaining an outboard body position to keep the rig sheeted in.

Gybe

In non-blasting situations, beachstarts or gybing where the rig is not completely sheeted in, still use the down element of Power to increase control over the rig and TRIM the board.

If you find you often lose control, stop suddenly or have difficulty maintaining speed, direction and stability, it is often down to sheeting out too suddenly, standing too upright or not having your harness lines far enough back.

STANCE - How to use your Body

The elements of VISION, TRIM, BALANCE and POWER help maintain the sailing line. TRIM keeps the board flat, BALANCE forms the framework of so many of our actions and POWER represents the very specific action of sheeting the boom in, back and down. STANCE reinforces and encapsulates the rest of the formula whilst having a significant impact on the effectiveness of our technique.

It's really important to realize that you're not riding upright on a board in a fixed position. Windsurfing is a dynamic sport that needs commitment together with the ability to adapt to changes in wind, water state and equipment. Windsurfing shouldn't be about upper-body strength or using the arms. The key to controlling the rig and board is how you use, align and direct specific forces through your torso, hips, legs and feet.

General tips

- Adopt a relaxed grip on the boom, with thumbs placed alongside fingers.

- Avoid high elbows, heavily flexed arms, breaking (bending forward) at the waist and standing too upright.

- Providing the arms remain extended, the option of an over or underhand grip with the front hand are both acceptable. However always adopt an overhand grip with the back hand.

Techniques

The secret of the number 7!

Essentially you use this number 7 shaped Stance for general cruising about. Use the first four elements of the Formula to form the shape of a number 7 with your body.

VISION – look forward over your front shoulder.

TRIM – front leg should be straighter and pointing forwards with back leg flexed to suit all sailing conditions.

BALANCE – (Pic 2) extend both arms (especially the front one) to keep the shoulders outboard to oppose the rig.

Pic 2

POWER – place the rear arm about a shoulder's width apart from the front arm which moves the body position outboard and helps sheet the rig in with the body weight.

Acceleration = Straight 7 Lift & Lock [out of harness]

When sailing along, you may feel power from the sail reduce, as this happens, switch to a Straight 7 stance to help maintain speed or acceleration.

> **Top Tips**
>
> - Narrow your hand spread to within shoulder width (and foot spread if out of the straps).
> - Fully extend the body and tighten the torso/ stomach by lifting and locking the hips.
> - Push through the toes to help TRIM.

Straight 7 in harness

Need Acceleration?

Switch into a really Straight 7 stance just after hooking in, getting in the straps, heading upwind or to keep planing through a lull. Tighten the torso. Extending and stiffening the torso transfers the forces through the body more effectively. Slouching inboard when the wind drops or if the board slows down is a windsurfing handbrake.

Top Tip

- Try actually pushing the boom away, rather than pulling on the arms.

Controlling Acceleration = Super 7 Drop and **Dig**

The other end of the STANCE range is called the Super 7 and is used in more dynamic situations. It is particularly relevant in higher wind speeds because it reinforces the TRIM and POWER elements of the Formula. When the board leaps about too fast and wildly, switch gear towards a Super 7 drop and dig. It should feel that the body, led by the hips, moves down and out, pushing and resisting against the windward rail with equally weighted feet. The hips move quite a lot when out of the harness, but if you're hooked in the action of trying to drop the hips is key.

As the wind increases we need to keep the board flat on the water. We can do this by dropping the hips, which will put more weight down through the boom and consequently the mast base. Weighting the heels will help lock the windward rail down as the board accelerates. This is particularly useful when setting up for the harness, foot straps or planing fast on the water.

Blasting control

When in the footstraps and harness, Super 7 drop and dig is accentuated. The body weight really sinks down and out in the harness, the back leg flexes and the front leg extends with the toes of the front foot pulling up in the strap to weight the heels and TRIM the board flat.

Super 7 drop and *push*

Sometimes you need to adopt a dynamic Super 7, but rather than dig the heels, you need to push through the toes. This is either to encourage acceleration for early planing, getting going or, to driving the board downwind into a gybe and for coming out of a tack.

Top Tips

- Widen your hand spread to just past shoulder width (and foot spread if out of the straps).
- Keep front leg extended to push hips well outboard.
- Drop the hips down by bending the back leg.
- Dig the heels to hold the windward rail down, pull up on the toes, especially in the front strap.
- Hunch the upper body slightly to accentuate the drop and dig action.

Gybe Set Up

Before and after unhooking, sink into a Super 7 drop and push stance by extending the front leg to turn the board off the wind.

Gybe Exit

Just before and after rotating the rig, the Super 7 drop and push drives the board flat and forward in the water, encouraging you to pull down on the boom.

Familiar comments when learning:

- "I didn't realise how much weight was needed in the harness"
- "I thought I was outboard"
- "I thought my back leg was bent"

So much of your progression is down to confidence and commitment. So don't be afraid to really commit and accentuate the stance actions.

Coach's Corner

Why doesn't the rig support me when I lean back?

This could be too small sail size for the conditions (especially wind strength), bending the arms too much or not sheeting in with the backhand to maintain Power.

Why can't I control the speed?

It's very easy to pull too much on the boom with both arms. Try to keep the rig still, relax the shoulders and let your body weight sink down and out in the harness.

Why does the board leap out of the water?

This could be down to an over-straightened back leg, not committing enough weight into the harness, pulling up on the toes in the front strap or too large a fin for the conditions (for more details see fin set up on page 26).

Intermediate Windsurfing Equipment

Moving on from the beginner stages of the sport happens pretty swiftly with regular practice. For an intermediate windsurfer it is important to understand how your equipment works and how to look after it both on and off the water. Making sure you have the right windsurfing gear is an ongoing consideration and one with which your instructor can help you. Avoid spending unnecessary amounts of money on too much or the wrong equipment. This chapter will help guide you through the equipment you will need and the terminology used.

Wetsuits

Something you are probably fairly familiar with by now, are usually made from neoprene and are available in different thicknesses, styles and colours. They are designed to provide some insulation to the body by trapping a thin layer of water between the body and the suit, which is warmed up by body heat. It should fit comfortably when bending and allow freedom of movement around the neck. Ensure the suit is of suitable thickness and design for the air and water temperature you intend to sail in.

Most manufacturers currently use a mixture of two materials, single lined usually used for the body and arms and double lined where an increase of durability is required such as the legs.

Single Lined Neoprene

One layer of nylon with the outside of the neoprene being smooth rubber. The nylon on the inside of the wetsuit provides durability while the smooth outer skin repels water quickly – reducing wind chill, increasing flexibility and reducing weight.

Double Lined Neoprene

A rubber with a layer of nylon laminated onto both sides, providing strength and durability. The disadvantage of this is loss of efficiency from wind chill from the water held on the outer surface of the material.

The disadvantage to a single lined or 'smooth skin' wetsuit is the vulnerability to nicks and tears due to the unprotected outer surface.

The most common types available are:
Shortie, Short Arm Steamer, Steamer

Accessories

Harness

There are two main choices of harness, the 'seat' harness or 'waist' harness.

Seat Harness

Seat or 'slalom' harnesses, sit around the hips and backside and have securing straps between the legs. This lower hook position forces the sailor to sit down more. Often chosen for larger sail freeride blasting and racing speedsters.

Waist Harness

Waist harnesses sit slightly higher on the body, the hook position should be around waist/belly button height. Comfortable on the back and easy to hook into. Make sure it fits properly and doesn't ride up when sailing!

Harness Lines

You can buy fixed or adjustable harness lines. We've given setting guidance in the Harnessing section (page 36). For a first time buyer, adjustable lines are most suited until you have a set preference for length.

Buoyancy Aids

When learning to windsurf it is important to wear a buoyancy aid. As you become more confident and able to use a harness, your instructor may give you the choice. However a buoyancy aid will build confidence when encountering planing conditions and waterstarts.

Other Accessories

Other pieces of equipment you may choose to increase your comfort when out on the water are: Neoprene shoes/booties, Rash vest, Gloves and a Hat.

Insurance

Always have third party insurance in case you have a close encounter with another windsurfer or water user. Check out www.rya.org.uk, it comes free as a benefit to any windsurfing member of the RYA!

Top Tips

- *Don't* buy harnesses too big.
- Choose a simple and good tightening system.
- The spreader bar should be pulled tight to the body – with no movement.

Intermediate Boards, Rig and Other Equipment

The Intermediate Board

- Lower in volume
- Slightly shorter and narrower
- Have footstraps fitted
- More responsive to foot and weight placement gives a more responsive ride.

The Intermediate Rig

- Sails are available in a larger range of sizes
- A greater number of battens
- Increase in defined aerofoil shape gives a more stable and responsive ride.

Other equipment

- Harness lines are fitted to both sides of the boom
- Harnesses are worn to enable you to hook into the lines

Greater power resulting in an increase of board speed due to a combination of all of the above.

Carrying a Board and Rig

It is important to be able to get your kit to and from the water safely without exhausting yourself. If it's a problem it usually means something isn't right, so stop and try to re-align the board and rig to the wind and have another go. With the right technique even the largest boards and rigs can be carried with relative ease to and from the water's edge.

With the wind blowing approximately side onto the board, place yourself between the board and the rig. Hold the boom with one hand (approx 30-40cm down the boom from the mast) and firmly grip either the rear footstrap or the windward forward footstrap with the other hand.

If you do have to carry the board and rig separately, always carry the rig with the mast pointing across the wind. Never leave the rig unattached and always make sure your board is on the shoreline first (tail into wind).

Board and rig on beach

Always position the board so that the rig lies downwind of the board in a safe and secure position.

Getting Sorted

Before heading out on the water always check your gear is in good working order. Spending a little time rigging correctly can make a huge difference to your comfort, safety and technique while on the water.

- Don't forget to sail safe
- Check the conditions
- Check your equipment
- Check yourself.

Whilst rigging, check that your:

- Fin bolt is tightened.
- Boom clamp, downhaul and outhaul are secure.
- UJ of your mastfoot is free from splits and cracks.
- Mastfoot, extension and uphaul are connected properly.
- Footstraps are screwed tightly and not twisting.
- Harness and lines are secure and not twisted.
- Board and rig are of an appropriate size for the conditions.

Gear Guide

Fin Size Formula

For early through to advanced Intermediates in non-planing and planing conditions.
Select a fin to keep you upwind and planing, but not too large to cause control problems.

Recreational or 'Freeride' boards 110-200L
Multiply your sail size by 5 and add 4 = Approximate fin size in cms. (e.g. 7m x 5 + 4 = 39cm fin)

Recreational or 'Freeride' boards below 110L in volume
Multiply your sail size by 5 and add 2 = Approximate fin size in cms. (e.g. 5m x 5 + 2 = 27cm fin)

Increase your fin size, between 1-4cm, if any of these are relevant
- You feel under-powered, slow to plane or are having difficulty staying upwind.
- You are using a board with a tail wider than 40cm (then add 4cm)
- The board is spinning out a lot (see page 49)
- You weigh over 85kg
- For exceptionally large rigs (9m+), or on boards with a width in excess of 75cm, you could increase fin size by up to 10cm.

Decrease your fin size, between 1-4cm, if any of these points are relevant:
- You feel overpowered while sailing
- The windward rail and/or nose of the board lifts up all the time
- You are under 70kg.

Mast Base

Set the mast base to help TRIM the board flat. These measurements are taken from the tip of the tail to the centre of the mast base and work on most modern boards.

Freeride boards 115-220L mast base range 130-145cm, average position - 135cm from the tail.

Freeride boards 95-115L mast base range 125-135cm, average position - 130cm from the tail.

Move the mast base back (usually 1-5cm from average setting) if the nose is digging through chop, or if the board feels unresponsive.

Move the mast base forward (usually 1-5cm from average setting) if the tail is sinking, the board is bouncing on the water, constantly luffing or you are using rigs 7m or more.

Boom Height

Sail cut outs for the boom vary and holding the rig up on the beach is a flawed method for setting the correct height before going on the water. The best method is to use the tail of the board as a reference. An average hands span off the back of the board more or less covers the whole range of sailor heights and will help give an approximate shoulder-high boom setting. Obviously the taller you are the higher the boom will go.

Low Boom

A low boom means the pull from the harness line is too horizontal. This forces the board sideways and will ruin your technique. The lines have to be in a position where they are pulling down on the boom.

In non-planing situations the boom should be top of shoulder/chin height - give or take a couple of centimetres.

5'0"-5'7" sailors would have the underside of the boom within 2-8cm of the tail.

A 5'8" sailor would have the boom's underside 2-5cm past the tail as pictured opposite.

5'8"-6'4" sailors would have the boom's underside up to 6-12cm past the tail. For first time experiences of getting into the footstraps use the more inboard training position. At the same time drop the boom (2-5cm from guide) because you are sailing in a position further forward and closer to the centreline. Remember that this position is just for that initial experience.

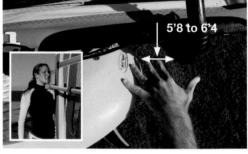

With wide (65cm+) Intermediate or Freeride boards, the boom needs to be set even higher (add 3-6cm to guide) because you need to move further away from the centreline to get to the straps. This will feel very high until you are positioned further outboard and closer to the straps. If you do stand the rig up on the beach the boom should be just around chin height for planing conditions.

Using the Daggerboard

In very light winds a daggerboard adds extra grip and consequently helps you point closer to the wind.

In light winds it is best to keep the daggerboard down on all points of sail, this will assist with stability and aid sideways resistance.

Daggerboard ←

Top Tips

- With the daggerboard down, drive through straight legs and toes to encourage the board to tilt onto the leeward rail giving extra grip - railing. In light winds this might mean having the toes over the centreline onto the leeward side of the board. In stronger winds both feet move towards the windward rail to control excessive railing.

- In planing conditions it is easier to sail across or away from the wind without the daggerboard, so retract the daggerboard if you're likely to get planing.

- When it comes to gybing, always retract the daggerboard unless you are trying an older style gybe, for example a flare gybe.

As the wind increases, and the board begins to plane, the board must be trimmed flat to maintain stability therefore the daggerboard should be lifted. If the daggerboard is left down it will try to 'lift' itself towards the wind, thus causing the windward rail of the board to angle-up out of the water and the stability of the board will be lost. In planing conditions without the daggerboard we rely on the wetted area, rails and fin to aid directional stability and to avoid slipping downwind.

Launching & Landing

Beachstart Technique

Here are three key skills that lead you quickly towards beach starting. As your confidence grows, move further into the water and try deeper beach starts.

Rig Elevation

Get into the habit of sliding the mast to windward as you elevate the rig above your head. If you try to lift or push the mast straight up above your head, the clew tends to catch or stay in the water.

1

2

3

4

Rig Twisting

To create lift from the rig the front arm should be thrust up and forward as the backhand pulls the boom in above your head. It feels like turning a set of giant handlebars above your head. This should create a twisting action that generates lift which needs to be accentuated in lighter winds or deeper water.

Bending the back leg and rolling the head inboard below the boom and towards the mast base is paramount for both beachstarts and waterstarts later. The front foot only comes up onto the board after Rig Twisting and Nose Over Toes actions have started.

Steering Prior to a Beach Start

Steering Downwind

To turn downwind and increase power, move the mast tip forward towards the nose by pushing down with the front hand (a) and pulling in and up on the backhand (b).

Steering Upwind

To turn upwind and reduce power, move the mast tip back towards the tail by pulling in on the front hand and pushing out on the backhand.

Top Tips

- Place the rear heel to windward of the centreline, between the straps and pointing across and slightly forwards on the board, really extend your front arm to prevent hugging the boom.
- Take your time leaving the front leg in the water for stability.
- Avoid lifting the hips and front leg up too soon.
- Never bring the head above the boom until the board is really moving.
- Not bending the back leg, sinks the tail, tends to turn the board into wind and also makes it much harder to come up onto the board, below the boom. Coming up with the head above the boom leads to either being propelled forwards (being catapulted) in strong winds or falling back into the water in light winds.

Beach Starting Sequence

With the board pointing slightly upwind of a beam reach, elevate the sail above your head.

Place the back foot up onto the board, bending the rear knee to help TRIM and pull the tail towards you.

Use the rig twist, taking the rig forward by extending the front arm and pulling in and up with the backhand above your head. Then roll your head down and towards the mast base underneath the boom, 'Nose Over Toes' as the rig continues up and forward.

Re-adjust and sail away.

Coach's Corner

Why do I get pulled over the front of the board?

This usually means the board is pointing too far downwind and the body has swung around the front of the board. May also be due to an over-extended back leg.

Why do I fall back into the water?

Often due to bending both arms, pulling the rig towards you and not getting the head rolling forward under the boom.

Why do I keep heading up into wind and/ or falling off the back?

You may simply be starting too far into wind. Use a little more aggression when moving the rig forward, making sure the back foot/leg isn't too far back, too straight or over-weighted is key.

Landing

Head upwind to reduce speed, pull down on the boom and step off to windward with the front foot first.

1

2

3

4

Coach's Corner

Waterstarts

If you keep developing your beachstarting skills it won't be long before you can start to use the rig to support you body in deeper and deeper water, maybe even lifting your feet off the ground in preparation for the waterstart.

Uphauling

Sometimes you can't beachstart or the rig is perfectly positioned to be uphauled. To improve stability start with the nose pointing slightly into the wind and/or chop. When the rig is drawn forwards you will be able to sheet the sail in more easily.

1

2

3

4

Top tip for higher wind or lower volume uphauling

- Turn the board 15-25 degrees upwind of a beam reach

Harnessing

Using the body weight in the harness, rather than arm strength, is the objective for every windsurfer.

Harness Line Positioning

It is impossible to state where exactly on the boom the harness lines should go. Fine-tuning on the water is essential for final adjustments. Ask your instructor to sail your equipment to ensure the lines are correctly set up. Additionally, here are two rough guides to help you get close to a decent harness line setup before going afloat. Don't forget, however that you must fine-tune on the water when you take short breaks in the shallows.

Rule of Hands

A simple guide for sails between 5-7m in light to marginally powered conditions. Match the number of clenched hands to the sail size and count them down the front of the boom: this is where the most forward harness-line fixing should be positioned. 5m rig - count five hands down the boom / 6m = 6 hands. This is only a very rough guide.

Rule of Thirds

Run a tape measure from the clew of the sail to the middle of the mast. Position the rear harness line fixing one third of the way down the boom. This result will be a comfortable sailing position and a well-tuned and powered rig, for fast blasting conditions.

Harness Line Width and Length Range

The objective is to create a good distance between the boom and the upper body improving your balance and stance.

Fix the buckles approximately a hand's width apart.

Elbow to wrist usually favours seat harness users.

Elbow to middle of the palm usually favours waist harness users.

Techniques

It is vital to prepare yourself for using the harness, you need to ensure that the five FORMULA skills are in place before hooking in.

Harness Planing

Vision and Trim

Use your newly acquired VISION and steering skills, to sail slightly closer to the wind than on a beam reach. This will encourage the rig, and the harness line to move to a more windward position prior to hooking in and will help to control excess speed and avoid catapults.

Get settled, position the feet to trim the board flat, extend the front leg and bend the back leg.

With the front arm extended, drop down into a Super 7 stance and pull in, back and down on the boom.

Bring the harness line towards you. In stronger winds really accentuate this action.

Hooking In

To hook in: use a short pull on the boom to swing the line towards you whilst simultaneously lifting the hips. While you might briefly glance at the lines or disrupt your stance, try to use VISION by looking forward again as soon as possible.

Once hooked in relax the arms, hold the rig still and sit down in the harness to keep pressure downwards in the line. This should enable you to establish a good stance.

Coach's Corner

On-water Tuning

- Place both hands on top of the lines while comfortably sailing along in the harness and with the rig sheeted-in and correctly trimmed.

- If the front arm feels more of a pull from the rig than the back – move both the line fixings forward.

- If the back arm feels more of a pull from the rig than the front – move both the line fixings back. Continue to make these small adjustments until both arms feel an equal and comfortable pull from the rig.

The harness lines too far back if

- The front hand is constantly pulling or having to be placed too far forwards on the boom.

- The apex of the harness line is angled forwards when sheeted in.

The harness lines too far forward if

- The back hand is constantly pulling or having to be placed too far back down the boom.

- The apex of the line is angled backwards when sheeted in.

Why can't I get near the harness line?

This is caused by sailing too far downwind and being too sheeted out. Head upwind and sheet the rig in.

Why do I keep heading up into wind?

Usually due to placing too much weight on the back foot, sheeting the rig in too much or bending both arms too much.

Why do I get pulled forwards or catapulted over by the rig?

You are either too far downwind when hooking in, or not committing enough weight in a downwards movement into the harness. Don't stand too upright.

Why do I fall in to windward?

You may be pulling too much on the front arm and sheeting out with the backhand, bending both legs rather than just the back one or leaning back too much.

Top Tips

- In lighter winds, move towards a Straight 7 stance – lift and lock stance after hooking in.
- In stronger winds, move towards a Super 7 stance – drop and dig to emphasize POWER and control acceleration.
- If powered up, head closer to the wind (upwind) to make hooking in easier and to help to avoid catapults.
- Once hooked in use the harness – think hips not hands.

Getting Going and Early Planing

We all want to get going as efficiently as possible. If you lose speed or control when hooking in, or are slow to plane, working through these points should dramatically improve your planing potential.

Techniques

Before even trying to get going, look forward and head upwind. This will help sheet the rig in, you will also need to bring the feet forward.

When settled, sink into a Super 7 drop and push stance. Depending on the conditions, continue by following the light or strong wind trim guide (see below).

Light Wind Trim

In light or marginal conditions to promote planing steer the board between 5-15 degrees downwind of a beam reach. The secret is to keep both feet forward and push through the toes of the forward facing front foot.

Strong Wind Trim

In stronger winds, head slightly upwind 5-15 degrees above a beam reach. This will help to control excessive acceleration and make hooking in easier. At high speeds or on wide high volume boards the back foot can move as far back as the rear straps. But be careful not to sink the tail while doing so.

Trim/Counterbalance/Power and Stance

Now it's time to get physical. Really accentuate the Super 7 drop and push stance and to keep the mast forward. This helps trim the board flat and enables the body to lean back and create a dynamic position to drive through an extended, forward-facing front leg. This can involve flexing the back leg to approximately 90 degrees. It should feel like you are falling backwards with your feet in front of you.

With the rig forward and powering up, sink the hips and flex the rear arm to pull in, back and down on the boom, to drive the board flat, to sheet the rig in and to bring the harness line to a more windward position prior to hooking in.

Coach's Corner

How do I control excess speed?

Head upwind, move further back and outboard adopting a Super 7 drop and dig stance before and after getting into the harness or footstraps.

Why do I slow down, stop planing or lose control before hooking in?

If you stand up and/or sheet out, all the rig's forces go down through the feet and the board stalls. You may also get pulled forward by the rig.

Footstraps

To achieve a smooth transition into the straps, you need to be planing at a good speed whilst applying all the elements of the Formula. You must also accentuate Counterbalance to help maintain TRIM and enable you to un-weight your feet (see Footstraps pics).

Technique

Front strap

Getting into the front strap the body must sit back to un-weight the front foot, therefore to compensate the rig must remain, or be moved forward. Remember to maintain Counterbalance the body moves one way as the rig moves the other.

Front Strap = Body Back & Rig Forward

VISION – Look and sail across the wind, or slightly closer to the wind (upwind) if well powered-up. Avoid all temptation to look at your feet!

TRIM – Place the front foot just forward of the front strap. In lighter winds, the back foot is placed just behind the front strap. In stronger winds it is placed towards the back strap.

BALANCE – To move the front foot, sit back and down over a bent back leg. Oppose this movement by slightly inclining the rig forward by extending the front arm.

POWER and STANCE – Keep the weight in the harness but don't pull the boom too close to the body. In marginal winds straighten your 7 stance. In stronger winds drop and dig towards a Super 7 stance.

Once in the front strap, get into the appropriate 7 stance and sail. Don't go for the back strap until you are comfortable getting the front foot in and out of the front strap. When you are ready, sail upwind slightly in preparation for the back strap.

Technique

Back strap

To be able to get into the back strap the body must lean forwards slightly enabling you to un-weight the back foot. The rig must either remain where it is or be moved back to compensate. Note: you cannot see how the board is heading upwind to create a safe environment in which to lean forward. In lighter winds leaning forward helps trim the board flat and obviously un-weights the back foot. In stronger winds heading upwind tames speed and helps you to overcome any fear of moving the back foot!

Back Strap = Head upwind Rig Back & Body Forward

VISION – Look forward and upwind to sail 5-15 degrees higher than a beam reach. Again, avoid all temptation to look at your feet!

TRIM – Place the back foot just in front of the back strap with the heel on the windward rail.

BALANCE – Rake the rig backwards to control speed and to establish the counterbalance to allow the body to lean forward and un-weight the back foot.

POWER – As the back foot slips into the back strap, sink down in the harness to help trim and maintain control.

STANCE – Once in the strap, re-establish a good stance and, if your speed has dropped, bear away.

Coach's Corner

When learning to get in the straps or if the conditions become more challenging, you may find that the board doesn't always oblige. Often one simple point can sort out what might feel like an almighty struggle. Essentially problems occur due to the movements of the feet, and consequently the body, which may throw everything out of kilter. So try all you can to keep the weight down in the harness and not pulling on the arms, to keep the rig sheeted in. Make slow movements and really avoid looking at the footstraps, while looking ahead to hold a steady straight course.

It's worth looking at the fault analysis in the next chapter - Blasting Control (p48).

Why do I head into wind when going for either front or back strap?

You may have too much weight on the back foot and not enough commitment to the harness in order to keep the rig stable and sheeted-in, thus directing a force down through the mastfoot. The rig and body are both leaning back at the same time, so try to move the rig in the opposite direction to the body:

> Front strap = rig forward, body back
> Back strap = rig back, body forward

Why do I end up missing the strap?

NEVER stand on a footstrap. Keep the toes touching the deck right next to the strap. Lift the heel and slide, don't stab. This compresses its structure which makes it very difficult to get the foot in it.

Why do I get catapulted going for the back strap?

Your sailing line is too far away from the wind downwind. Head the board slightly closer to the wind, by steering with your feet and raking the rig back. You can then lean slightly forward to un-weight the back foot safely.

Why does my back foot trail in the water?

This could be due to the strap not being set up properly and not open enough (see page 26 for setup) or, if you are wearing boots, they may be too bulky. Your heel should be on the windward rail.

Blasting Control

Is all about trying to maintain a flat board, a sheeted-in rig with the body balanced firmly outboard in the harness. The ideal body position is with the hips resisting the pull from the rig and with equal weight distribution through each leg and very little pull in on the arms. Holding this position may be challenging in changeable wind speeds and water states. The ability to alter stance and reinforce the other elements of the Formula enable you to maintain speed and control of equipment.

To help you understand more about blasting control, here are the most common scenarios that you are likely to encounter and tips on how to deal with them.

Techniques
To accelarate

Whenever you feel the board slow, you need to immediately switch stance towards a Straight 7 by lifting and locking the hips.

Remember to tighten the torso!

TRIM – Push through the toes (especially the front foot) to drive the board flat.

BALANCE – Front arm fully extends, as the shoulder leans back to counterbalance the upright mast.

POWER – Maintain weight in the harness and keep the rig sheeted in.

Maintaining speed in lulls

Good trim and accentuated counterbalance are essential

To trim the board flat, the upper body must lean right forward, sometimes slightly bending the front leg to accentuate the forward lean. To counterbalance, the rig is kept in a raked back position and sheeted in to maintain power.

If you swing inboard, slouch and hang heavily off the boom, you'll often sink the tail, causing you to slow even more.

To stop spinning out

At high speeds over choppy water the fin can lose grip and spin out, (the fin loses its grip in the water and the whole board slides sideways). This is due to either, a sudden change of direction, the windward rail lifting or excessive weight on the back leg. The moment the nose lifts, heavily flex the back leg. If the fin does spin out, sheet the sail out slightly and then use the back foot to pull or snap the tail in under the body to re-engage the fin.

Top Tips

- A narrow hand spread on the boom helps you to lean forward.
- If the water ahead has wind on it - dark patches, then bear away to promote acceleration.
- If the water ahead is looking flat, glassy or windless then head upwind using the tips above, you'll pick the next gust up sooner and at least you'll be upwind if you stop completely for a while. Don't bear away into a lull as you'll lose ground and be sailing away from the wind and therefore away from the next gust.

Control excessive speed over chop whilst blasting along

Accentuate the Super 7 drop and dig stance. Sink your hips down in the harness to help emphasize power and dig the heels down into the windward rail to improve trim. Sometimes this requires the upper body to hunch slightly. Heavily flexing the back leg is important in preventing the nose from lifting.

BALANCE – Directly oppose the rig, but keep a good distance from the mast with a strong extended front arm.

POWER – Accentuate pulling in, back and down on the boom to help TRIM.

TRIM – Dig your heels in by pulling up on the toes in the straps.

Avoiding getting catapulted

- Avoid sailing too far downwind at speed, over-extending the front leg or dropping your VISION down too much.
- Don't attempt to get into the harness and/or footstraps when sailing fast across the wind or downwind. Head upwind a little to reduce speed first.
- Counterbalance the forward pull in the rig by committing the body weight back, down and into the harness.
- Move the feet further back on the board if you're out of the straps.

Why you head up into wind

- By dropping your vision and looking down too much – otherwise known as gear gazing.
- By placing too much weight on, or over, a straightened back leg.
- By unbalancing yourself thanks to pulling the rig too close to the body or leaning the body and rig back at the same time.

To slow down

- If you ever feel out of control, head upwind. (see planing steering page 54 for more details).

Top Tips

- Make sure the sail isn't tuned to provide too much power.
- Check your harness lines are far enough back on the boom.
- Make sure your fin is not too small. Check the fin guide on page 26.

Steering and Sailing Upwind and Daggerboard

It's all very well being able to blast about but you want to be able to steer smoothly and safely in both lower and higher speeds, therefore enabling you to direct your board up or downwind directly into tacks and gybes. You'll see that in all cases we rely heavily on your VISION, Counterbalance and STANCE range to do this. Your actions need to be quite dynamic at low speeds and more subtle at higher speeds.

Techniques

Nonplaning steering upwind
Altering course, preparing to get going in lighter winds, or when preparing to tack.

First and foremost use your vision to look upwind.

As you do so apply some specific trim to the windward rail (the rail closest to the wind) by sinking down, back and outboard). Using a Super 7 'drop and dig' stance will help with leaning the whole rig towards the tail (often referred to as raking the rig back).

As the board heads into wind, bring both feet forward again to oppose the rearward raked rig.

Coach's Corner

Why do I head straight into wind?
Often due to a continually over-weighted back foot and leaning both the rig and body back too far for too long.

Nonplaning steering downwind

A skill really worth accentuating and becoming proficient at. It will not only help set up for early planing but also links into gybe entries and exits.

Look downwind and spread your stance on the board and hand grip on the boom.

Flex your back leg to sink into a Super 7 drop and push stance.

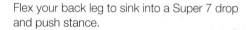

Drive through the toes of the extended front leg and counterbalance the rig as it leans forward.

Top Tip
- With a bent back arm sheet the sail in extending the front arm as the mast leans forward. Try to pull the back foot underneath you to help turn the board.

Sailing upwind off the plane

Whenever you leave the shore, get caught in a lull or find yourself coming on and off the plane, your first reaction should be to head upwind. Even without a daggerboard it will be possible to point closer to the wind.

Looking upwind over that front shoulder, use specific trim by heavily depressing the windward rail with the forward facing front foot. The rig needs to be raked back to steer the board upwind, then once the board is tilted, it will be possible to bring the rig forward with a fully extended front arm to maintain a good counterbalance position.

Planing steering

When blasting along in the harness and footstraps, it takes only the slightest pressure to alter course. The more outboard you are it's easier to oppose the movement of the rig to push and pull through the legs to help change the board's direction.

Upwind planing steering

Really useful skill when trying to reduce speed, prepare for a tack, sail upwind for longer distances. In non-planing and planing situations, weighting the windward rail is key to keeping the board trimmed flat.

Hanging low in a Super 7 stance, towards the back of the board. Weighting the heels on the windward rail will turn the board upwind.

Looking over the front shoulder at speed can turn the board upwind. Pulling up on the toes and digging the heels (especially the front foot) will dig and weight the windward rail into the water and the board will head upwind.

The rig is being raked back, your front arm extended and the upper body leaning right forward to counterbalance and maintain trim. By narrowing the grip and bringing both hands slightly forward on the boom, helps oppose the rearward raked rig.

Downwind planing steering

Turning downwind helps increase speed and prepares you for planing entries into a gybe.

Provided the rig is well sheeted-in, the board is flat and you are in an outboard body position in a good stance, turning downwind takes very little effort. Essentially pushing through the toes of an extended front leg and flexing the back leg is enough to drive the board downwind.

If you also extend the front arm to force the rig forward, the board really turns away from the wind.

Coach's Corner

While sailing upwind all the plane, why does the board slip sideways, stop and go backwards?

This is due to not having enough tilt on the rail, excessive weight on the back foot or over-sheeting with the backhand.

When steering downwind in non planning conditions, why won't the board turn?

Real accentuation is so often needed, so make sure you are low and the rig is twisted forward.

Top Tips

- Make sure the back leg truly bends, otherwise the board won't turn downwind or you may catapult.
- In stronger winds pull down hard on the boom to control power and sink the body low towards the tail of the board in a Super 7 drop and push stance.

Fast Tacking

A fast, dry tack can be a fluid, secure and totally achievable skill in all conditions. Your existing tack now needs to progress into a smoother, more continuous and speedier turn. It's very easy to pick up bad habits on very high volume beginner boards. To combat this we've highlighted not only what improves tacks, but also what enables you to achieve them in stronger winds and on lower volume boards.

Techniques

Essentially tacking relies on VISION, always creating a Counterbalance and using specific footwork, which we call shifting and switching. Each skill is fundamental for successful tacks at all levels.

VISION

Look and sail upwind before tacking, the head should then spin to look out of the turn as soon as possible.

Counterbalance

For many, the defining part of the tack is realising the importance of always opposing the rig's forces, position and movement with your body. Not only should you keep the mast away from you, but if the rig is moved one way the body must move the other way. 99% of dismounts occur if this opposing theme is neglected. This is especially true at the difficult midway point of the tack while trying to whiz round an upright mast and end up pulling the rig towards them or falling onto the sail.

> **Top Tips**
> - Try a few tacks just looking where you want to go.
> - Try to avoid looking at the feet, hands or directly at the sail.

Footwork - shifting and switching

Practise the following exercise on land or on a large board.

From your normal sailing position.

Step forward, wrapping the front foot tightly around the mast.

Shift your weight onto your front foot.

The back foot shifts behind the front foot and towards the nose of the board.

The new back foot steps as far down the new side of the board as possible.

The new front foot is positioned behind the mast and we sail away.

Now let's combine and accentuate VISION, Counterbalance and shifting and switching for a secure fluid tack.

VISION – Unhook and come out of the straps if you're in them and look and sail upwind. As you rake the rig, place your front hand on the mast.

Shifting and Switching – The front foot must step forward and wrap around the mast base before the board is head to wind.

Counterbalance – As the board sails upwind, move the body and rear foot forward and inboard. It's important to keep the rig-raking movement going, so that the clew crosses just over the tail of the board, this indicates that you have passed through the eye of the wind. It should feel like you're dropping the rig back, rather than pulling too hard on the boom. The secret here is to edge the hips inboard so they face towards the *back* of the board *before* making your move to switch the feet.

These next points happen almost simultaneously, one continuous movement should be your goal.

VISION – Once the board passes right through the eye of the wind, look out of the turn and grab the boom on the new side with the new front hand.

Shifting and Switching – The old back foot switches in closely behind the front foot towards the nose of the board.

Counterbalance – Tacks become successful or otherwise at this point. Push the mast to a leeward position as you switch the feet and move the body to an upwind or windward position.

BALANCE – The old mast hand is released once the new front hand is placed on the boom. Step as far down the board as possible and sharply incline the rig forward to counterbalance.

VISION – Enjoy the view of your new direction.

Super 7 – Adopting a wide stance on your feet enables you to push the board away from the wind - dropping, pushing and get going.

Coach's Corner

Dismounts are usually due to either pulling the rig too close to the body, moving in the same direction as the rig, not moving the feet or looking at the board – gear gazing!

Why do I fall into windward with the sail before I go round the mast?

You may not be getting the hips and back foot far enough inboard and towards the mastfoot.

Why does the nose sink and I fall off the front?

Your feet may be too far forward, towards the nose of the board, or you are trying to go round an upright mast.

I get to the other side and fall in with the sail on top of me?

The board wasn't turned far enough through the wind during the initial steering phase of the tack and this was not followed by a pushing of the mast to leeward.

Gybing

Good gybing requires polished technique and precise timing, a fundamental windsurfing manoeuvre that can be as frustrating when you get it wrong or invigorating when you nail it. Unless the right technique is understood from the beginning, your potential for success will be limited. What follows is a highlighting of the key skills that can help to formulate a reliable gybing technique for every style of board and wind strength.

The non-planing carve gybe (known as the npcg) stems from the planing step-gybe where the feet are changed before the rig flips. The skills that follow can be used for your first ever gybes or as training to take the myth, confusion and much of the difficulty out of the elusive planing 'carve gybe'. It's important to state that the techniques outlined here cross over between non-planing and planing conditions. As you become more experienced in the application of these skills you will be able to implement them at greater speed and in more challenging conditions. If you are currently having difficulty with gybing then these skills are a great way to get back to basics with a view to later applying them in more advanced situations.

The gybe has been stripped down into simple component parts to help you to focus on each skill to help you to rebuild the whole manoeuvre into a smooth and dry transition.

Techniques

You'll see how we apply VISION and Counterbalance throughout the gybe as well as adopting a committed Super 7 drop and push stance for the entry and exit of the manoeuvre.

We now need to add in two specific transitional skills that are fundamental to the success of non-planing and planing gybes: Shifting and Switching for effective carving and reliable foot change; The Rig Rotator to control the forces, position and movement of the rig during the middle to end of the gybe.

Shifting and Switching

If the hips are not shifting into the turn and the feet don't switch smoothly, you reduce your chances of success. Here's how it works:

Shifting

Place the toes just on the inside of the rail in front of the back strap. The rear hip shifts sideways across the board into the turn, weighting the back foot by bending at the knees and flexing the ankles.

Switching

With the hips shifting into the turn, the rig is kept forwards and towards the outside of the turn to counterbalance. As the board just passes the dead downwind stage of the gybe, the old front foot switches across the board heel to toe in front of the back foot.

Switched

The new front foot steps immediately forward. At this point it is imperative to bend the new back leg to adopt a Super 7 drop and push stance. This keeps the hips back and maintains pressure on the windward rail to counterbalance and control the rig and drive the board forwards and trim it flat.

Top Tips

- Make sure the new back foot ends up on the edge of the board near the rear footstrap to maintain that all-important pressure on the inside rail.
- Look out of the turn during the hand change and as the rig is drawn forward.

Rig Rotator

The mast needs to be rotated downwind, back towards the tail and then forward in one smooth continuous action. Improve your muscle memory by practising your shifting and switching and rig rotator on land. If you keep the mast moving it takes the weight and strain out of the rig release.

Don't look at the rig, look forwards.

Clew Control

With the feet switched, look out of the turn where you want to head. The clew arm pulls in and down on the boom sheeting the clew in. As can be seen above the rig is directly across the middle of the board. Drop low into your Super 7 stance on a broad reach before rotating the rig.

Rig Release

Slide the front hand towards the mast before releasing the backhand. As the boom swings over the nose the mast hand guides and rotates the mast in a circular sweep towards the tail. The hips may shift slightly forward to counterbalance the rig.

Hand Change

The hand change happens when the rig is towards the tail of the board. Grab the boom with the new mast hand on the new side then sharply incline the mast forward. The action of rotating the mast back and then forward (but not to windward) brings the boom inboard making it easier to grasp the boom with the new clew hand and sheeting the sail in.

Super 7 exit

To complete the gybe, the body drops back, to oppose the forward pull of the rig, into a Super 7 stance giving maximum stability.

Coach's Corner

Don't cheat. You might get away with shuffling poorly placed feet, premature rig flips, standing too upright, gear gazing or lazy actions in lighter winds. Any of this scruffy technique will not do you any favours in stronger winds.

If you stand too upright, too far forward, sheet out or break at the waist, there's a high chance of being pulled over by the rig. Shifting your hips into the turn is key. This will oppose the movement of the rig, create counterbalance and encourage the board to turn.

Not sliding the front hand up towards the mast, standing up, or looking at the rig, means you have a greater chance of being pulled over when it rotates.

Pulling the mast too close to the body and to windward is a surefire way of messing up at the end of the gybe.

Clew-First Beach Start

A good way to become accustomed to the Rig Rotator is to practise clew-first beach starts. When sailing clew-first, keep the board on a broad reach and pull in and down hard with the clew hand.

1

2

3

Gybing technique
1. Entry

Vision Look into and through the turn.

Super 7 drop... Back hand right down the boom, then drop the hips.

...and push through an extended front leg to turn the board off the wind. This is helped if the front arm extends and the backhand sheets in a lot.

2. Mid Gybe

Counterbalance The hips are low and back, the mast is forward. As the board turns, the hips shift to the inside of the turn and the mast is leant to the outside.

The rear placed backhand *must* pull in and down on the boom (see clew first beach start - page 64).

At low speeds, don't tilt the board, just angle the mast, leaning it further to outside of the turn. Use **Shifting and Switching** footwork when the board is downwind, keep pulling down on the boom as the foot switch takes place.

3. Gybe Exit

Vision Wait! Look out of the turn as you sail clew first for a couple of seconds on a broad reach.

Rig Rotator Slide the mast hand down the boom and then drop the hips down to counterbalance the movement of the rotating rig.

Vision Look out of the turn before, during and after releasing the clew.

Super 7 Drop the hips and push through an extended front leg to drive the board forward on exit.

Top Tips

- Backhand should be well past rear the harness line.
- Position the rig as if splitting the board in half with the rig, this is acheived by sheeting the clew hand close to your head.
- Slide the mast hand down the boom towards the mast in readiness for the Rig Rotator.
- Ensure the hand change (from boom to boom) happens when the rig is towards the tail of the board mid Rig-Rotator.

Choosing the Right Board and Rig

Intermediate Boards

With so many different styles and sizes of board on the market, choosing a board can be a daunting task. You may wish to back this advice up by reading board tests, demo-ing equipment and discussing your requirements with retailers (who sail regularly) and others of a similar level. Avoid purchasing the first board you get offered. Neither should you base your decision on colour, brand or because 'it's cheap'! Your main considerations when buying a board are: volume, width and the appropriate style/type of board for your level and aspirations.

Intermediate Volume Guide

You have now reached the stage where you are considering buying your own board. The guide below should get you within 5-10L of the optimum board for your ability, weight and intended use in the conditions you will be windsurfing in.

1. Take your weight in kilos   eg.   80kg
2. Add rig weight when wet   10kg
3. Add board weight wet with mast base, straps and fin   10kg

                                             Total   100kg

4. Convert total weight (kg) into litres (L).   **100 litres**
5. Now add, or subtract from this amount by including one selection from each of the following three categories. For an example we will look at an intermediate person progressing towards footstraps and these figures have been highlighted.

Sailor ability

Improver – early intermediate	+50L
Intermediate (developing planing techniques)	**+30L**
Intermediate – advanced	+5L
(mastered footstrap/harness/waterstart/blasting)	

Intended use

Wave riding	-10L
Bump and jump coastal style	- 5L
Freeride blasting	0L
Feasible Freestyle	+ 5L
Marginal Wind Cruising about	**+10L**

Predominant wind conditions

flat water/lighter winds (9-15 knots)	**+20L**
Medium (15-22 knots)	0L
Strong (18-30 knots)	-10L

Example for an 80kg intermediate sailor developing planing skills, harness and footstraps.

1. Sailor 80kg + Board (10kg) + Rig (10kg)
= 100kg (convert to Litres)   100L
2. Sailor Ability - Intermediate   + 30L
3. Intended Use - Freeride Blasting   +10L
4. Predominant Wind Conditions 9-15 knots
                                    + 20L
Totals   **160L**

Total volume = 100+30+10+20 = **160L** (This would be ample volume to enable the 80kg sailor to uphaul)

Width

Board volumes are not always accurate. Width is another good way to judge a board's suitability.

Wider boards are in general

- More stable, able to plane earlier and able to carry larger fins and sails.
- More suited to heavier sailors or early planing.
- Bouncier in chop and harder to control when over-powered or at higher speeds.

Narrower boards are in general

- Slower to plane and work better with smaller fins and sails.
- Easier to control at speed or in chop, with increased directional stability.
- More suited to lighter sailors or stronger winds.

Types of Boards

1. Beginner-Improver Board

Volume range 170-220L
Length 260-290cm Width 80-90cm
Often fitted with a retractable daggerboard or central fin.

2. Large Freeride

Good option for ambitious early intermediates and inland intermediate-advanced sailors or those who prefer super-planing with large sails.
Volume range 135-170L
Length 250-270cm Width 65-80cm

(See photograph page 69)

3. **All Rounders**

Also known as smaller Freerides, Freemove, Crossover, Freestyle-Wave. Often chosen as a second board for higher winds.
Volume range 70-135L
Length 240-270cm Width 58-65cm

Freestyle

Not happy going in straight lines. They do, however, like corners, jumping and spinning and have a fin the size of a key ring.
Volume range 80-115L
Length 235-250cm Width 56-65cm

4. **Wave**

Experienced sailors like their manoeuvreability in rougher waters, higher winds and for carving tight turns on the face of a wave.
Volume range 60-100L
Length 235-250cm Width 52-57cm

5. **Speed**

Stiff, narrow and super fast.
Volume range 50-100L
Length 235-260cm Width 30-40cm!

Intermediate Rigs

Building a sail quiver

Having a range of sails (a quiver) enables you to windsurf in most wind conditions but this doesn't mean that you need a sail for all wind strengths. Learning to tune your rig, develop early planing skills, develop higher wind control and selecting the right quiver are all part of minimizing both the number of sails you need and the number of times you need to change sails during your time on the water.

Top Tips

- Go for realistic differences between sail sizes. For larger rigs (over 6m²) this can mean differences up to 2m². With rigs under 6m², the size difference should be between 0.5-1.0m².
- Buy wisely. Two sails in good condition, enable you to sail within a wide wind-range, and are better than three sails in poor condition which perform badly.
- Once committed to the sport, it's worth buying 2-3 sails together from the same manufacturer. You may get a better deal and they tend to rig and tune in a similar manner, giving a more consistent feel to your quiver.

Quiver chart and guide

For 1-2 boards allow for a variation of about 0.5-1.0m to suit your specific needs.

Level/location	Board	Stature	No. of sails	Suggested Sizes
Improver	170L+	65kg	2 sail quiver	5.0m/6.0m
Improver	170L+	85kg	2 sail quiver	5.5m/7.0m
Improver	170L+	65kg	3 sail quiver	5.0m/6.0m & 7m
Improver	170L+	85kg	3 sail quiver	5.5m/6.5m & 8m
Intermediate/Inland	140L+	65kg	2 sail quiver	5.5m & 7.5m
Intermediate/Inland	140L+	85kg	2 sail quiver	6.0m & 8.0m
Intermediate/Inland	140L+	65kg	3 sail quiver	5.0m/6.0m/8.0m
Intermediate/Inland	140L+	85kg	3 sail quiver	5.5m/7.0m & 8.5m

Rotational sails

As you progress and start to travel faster you will need a rig that has a better aerofoil shape and will provide you with greater stability and ease of handling. You will hear the term rotational applied to most recreational rigs used today and this refers to the way the battens are designed to set or rotate around the mast when the sail is powered up by the wind. This setting of the battens provides more of an aerofoil shape and gives the rig extra stability and better handling in a wider range of conditions. Rotational sails have between four-six battens and use considerable tension via the downhaul to help hold the shape of the sail and maintain its stability. You might hear other sails described as freeride, all-round, freestyle, freestyle-wave or wave, but they are all a variation of a typical five-batten rotational sail.

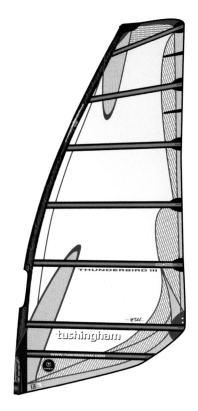

*This is a 'four-cam' sail
used for speed and racing.*

Variations of a rotational sail

Twin-cam sails are very similar to rotational sails, but have slightly larger luff tubes that accommodate a small, plastic cupping device that holds the end of the batten against the mast. These sails are designed to give the rig more of an aerodynamic and powerful shape at the point where the air travels over the luff tube.

Disadvantages of twin-cam sails are that they feel heavier at low speeds, the larger luff tubes tend to fill up with water when uphauling, beachstarting or waterstarting and they are harder to handle and rotate in tacks and gybes. In the hands of an experienced windsurfer, however, they are well-suited to full-power sailing in a straight line.

Sail materials

Some of the most common materials used in the construction of sails are

Monofilm – Seethrough material used on most modern rotational sails. A thicker form of Mylar® that does not require supporting layers. Light weight material enabling light, manoeuvrable sails to be constructed.

Dacron® – Basic sail cloth used widely in the construction of beginner sails because of its lightness. Commonly used as batten-pockets and luff tubes on rotational sails.

Mylar® – Thin film of plastic usually laminated onto a supporting layer such as mesh or crossed fibres.

X-ply® – Usually two sheets of Mylar® with a combination of fibres such as Spectra®, Kevlar® or carbon laminated between. The X pattern adds to the strength and tear resistance of the sail.

Masts

A good quality mast is a good investment. Skimping on the cost of a mast can have a negative impact on your windsurfing, as a cheap mast may be too stiff or heavy. When choosing a mast you should aim to match, as closely as possible, the recommendations printed on your sail and sail bag.

Types of mast

There are two types of mast on the market, a normal diameter mast or Skinny or RDM reduced diameter mast. Both are suited to the intermediate sailor. An RDM mast, whilst no lighter, will make rigs feel extremely light and manageable. They are best suited to sails below 6.5m² and are very popular with children, lighter sailors and more advanced freeride, wave and freestyle sailors. Masts are supplied in 2 pieces which slide together, a top section and a bottom section. Avoid purchasing a very old one-piece mast on the second-hand market; because of the size they are very difficult to transport.

Mast Length

The information printed on the sail and sail bag will help you to choose the correct length of mast, and there will be an optimum mast length for any given sail. Not everyone will wish or can afford to purchase one mast for each sail in their quiver, so an alternative mast length is recommended. In this way you may be able to use the same mast for more than one sail, making use of a mast extension (see page 75). Mast lengths are measured in cm and the range of masts available is 370 (for a very small wave sail), 400, 430, 460, 490, 520 and 550 (for a very large race sail). The most popular sizes sold for freeride sailing in the UK are 430 and 460. The mast length is linked to IMCS (see below).

Carbon content

Most modern masts are constructed from a mixture of fibreglass and carbon. The higher the carbon content within a mast, eg. 55-100%, the more responsive and lighter it will be. Lower carbon content masts tend to be around 30-50%, and are perfectly suited to the freeride environment. Higher carbon content, although lighter, is not essential and does come with a more expensive price tag. Again beware of very old second-hand masts which may be made solely of fibreglass. These are often very heavy, very stiff and can break down over time leaving you with fibreglass splinters in your hands.

IMCS (Indexed Mast Curve System)

This is an international standard for measuring how stiff a mast is. The IMCS recommendations are printed on your sail and sailbag, (ie. IMCS 25) and, as with the mast length selection, it is best to match the manufacturer's recommendations as closely as possible. In general, the longer the mast, the higher the IMCS number and, hence, the stiffer the mast.

Mast extension

An adjustable mast foot which fits into the bottom of your mast, enabling you to fit more than one sail in your quiver on to the same mast. They come in different lengths up to 50cm and are made from aluminum or carbon and available in standard and RDM diameters.

Booms

An aluminium or alloy boom is the most common choice of boom and is likely to be the style that comes with a board or rig package. For pure, unadulterated luxury choose a carbon boom which, although not always lighter, will be stronger and stiffer, helping to make the rig more stable. Carbon booms are often double the price of a regular alloy boom but worth the investment if you sail frequently or you are a heavier sailor using very large rigs which require a long boom.

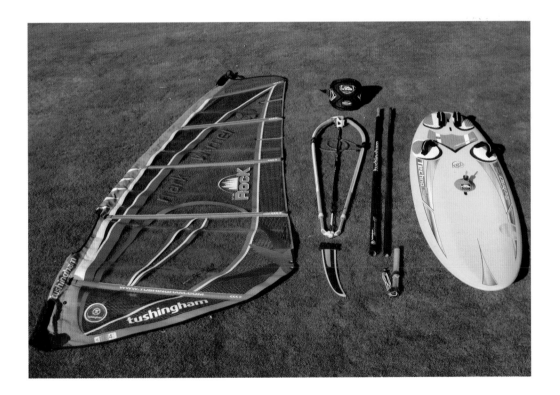

Rigging and Tuning

Even high performance sails can perform badly if they are not rigged well. So don't throw your rig together and go sailing, tune it. This may seem daunting at first but your instructor will take you through the steps. Practise rigging on no wind days, take your time and pay attention to the markings and measurements on the equipment. All this will help you to set your sail well helping to maximize your potential afloat.

Rigging sequence

Firmly connect the two piece mast, slide it to the top of the luff tube or head cap.

For the majority of recreational sails, apply downhaul until the leech is 'loose' or 'floppy' down to the third/fourth batten.

Attach boom tightly before fully applying downhaul.

Apply further downhaul and outhaul to the manufacturer's recommended mast and boom settings printed on the sail/sail bag.

Coach's Corner

Fullness & power

The fullness of the sail should be in the lower third, with the sail becoming flatter and twisting off towards the head and leech.

Less downhaul and outhaul increases 'fullness', and therefore increases the power in the sail, but reduces stability.

Extra downhaul and outhaul flattens the sail, reducing power and increasing stability.

Having to pull really hard on the outhaul to get the battens away from the mast usually means that insufficient downhaul has been applied. With the correct amount of downhaul you should only need 2-5cm of outhaul.

Tension the battens until the creases are just eliminated from either side of the battens. Beware of applying too much tension which can stress the battens into S-bending or even snapping.

Top Tips

- Use either your harness spreader bar or a rig puller to really get some tension on the downhaul.
- The battens above and below the boom should move, or 'rotate', around the mast with only slight resistance when using first finger and thumb.

How a Sail Works

How the wind, sail and board work together to create forward motion is a reasonably complicated procedure and one that, when blasting backwards and forwards on the water, many rarely consider!

Laminar and turbulent flow

You may have been instructed to sheet in your sail, the reason being an over-sheeted sail kills the power produced. As long as you sheet the sail to the correct angle of the wind, the airflow will be smooth on both sides and referred to as laminar flow and is something you will develop continually throughout your windsurfing.

If a sail in non-planing conditions is over-sheeted, for example when it is fully pulled into the centreline on a beam reach, the air is unable to flow along the sail efficiently. The air, in this case, would not only bounce-off the windward side but also break away from the leeward side. The result is inefficient and disturbed airflow – as turbulent flow. A run is another example of this and hence the reason for it being the slowest point of sail.

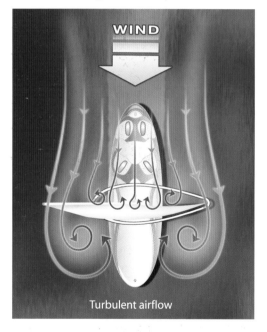

Turbulent airflow

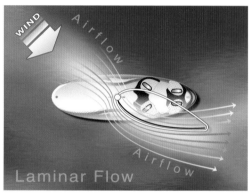

Laminar Flow

The Driving Force

As air flows around each side of a sail, differences in pressure are created, namely low pressure on the leeward side and high pressure on the windward side. This difference in pressure, which creates a force at 90° from the chord of the sail known as lift, would given the chance drive the board sideways and downwind. The board, however, does not like to be sailed sideways through the water so it resists doing so. It is this lateral resistance of the board's wetted area, fin and daggerboard that transfer the lift from the sail into the forward motion of the board.

Apparent Wind

The two winds you feel when out windsurfing are:

True Wind Existing or prevailing wind at the time - the wind you feel when standing still.

Induced wind Wind created by the forward movement of the board.

A combination of the true wind and the induced wind produces Apparent Wind. The wind you feel affects your equipment as you cruise along.

Example:
At rest in the secure position, you only feel the true wind. As you pull in the sail and create forward motion, an induced wind builds. It appears now that the wind has moved forward and increased whereas the wind you are feeling at this point is in fact a combination of the induced and true winds, known as the Apparent Wind.

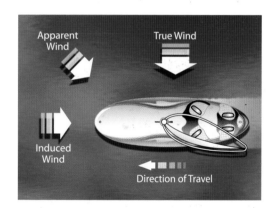

• As you accelerate, the Apparent Wind moves forward towards the induced wind, requiring you to sheet in more.

• As you slow down, the Apparent Wind moves back towards the true wind direction, requiring you to sheet out.

Coach's Corner

Sheeting in or correctly positioning the sail, is a fundamental aspect of planing windsurfing,

• At low speeds and when heading downwind (off the plane) the rig needs to be eased out slightly.
• When heading upwind, or when encouraging or maintaining planing speeds the sail needs to be pulled in.
• If the sail is under-or over-sheeted the laminar flow is compromised and the airflow becomes more turbulent causing the sail to lose its efficiency, stability and power.

Safety and Self-Rescue

Prevention rather than cure and the seven common senses

Generally windsurfing is very safe, especially if you are progressing at a RYA Centre where there are qualified instructors and safety boats on a carefully chosen stretch of water. Nevertheless, you should be aware of the fundamentals of how to help yourself both on and off the water should any problems arise. This knowledge will increase your confidence, helping you to make good progress in your windsurfing.

Prevention rather than cure

In windsurfing, as in any situation, it is always better to prevent a problem arising rather than stumbling into it and then trying to fix it.

The Seven Common Senses

1. Is all your equipment seaworthy and suitable?
   Clothing, board, rig and all essential spares

REMEMBER THE MOST COMMON NEED FOR RESCUE IS EQUIPMENT FAILURE!

2. Tell someone where you are going and when you will be back

3. Obtain a weather forecast for the local sailing area

4. Are you capable of handling the prevailing conditions?

IF IN DOUBT, DON'T GO OUT!

5. Windsurf with others

6. Avoid strong tides, offshore winds and poor visibility

7. Consider other water-users

Ways of Attracting Attention

If conditions or circumstances change and you are unable to return to the safety of the shore then take immediate action to attract the attention of either your instructor, a safety boat, another windsurfer or those on land.

- **International Distress Signal**

  Clench your fists and repeatedly raise and lower your arms at either side of your body, while kneeling or sitting on your board. Take care not to cross your arms above your head and to make these actions slowly to avoid exhaustion.

- **Waving a Dayglo flag or similar**

  Either a Dayglo flag, (available from www.rya.org.uk) bright material, hat or piece of clothing can be waved in the direction of a potential source of rescue. This can be incredibly effective, even over large distances.

- **Blowing a whistle**

  A useful way to attract the attention of those close by. However, if the wind is very strong, or in the wrong direction, the sound could get carried away. The repeated sounding of a whistle is one of several International Distress Signals, so should only be used in emergencies.

Methods of Self Rescue

The following methods become harder on lower volume boards, in rougher water and in stronger winds. However they may come in useful if there is no alternative rescue to hand.

- **Flagging**

  Standing either side of the mast with the mast in front of you (ie. In the secure position) is a very simple and easy way to drift or steer downwind.

- **Butterfly**

  In very light or no wind conditions, lay the rig over the back of the board, remove your harness hook, lie face-down on the board, use your feet to hold the rig in place and paddle with the arms.

- **Full de-rig**

  This is an extreme option and it is very difficult to keep hold of masts, extensions and booms unless you tie them down firmly. Another disadvantage is that you make yourself less visible when you de-rig the sail.

Turtle Rescue

- **Turtle**

  A trickier alternative to the Butterfly where the rig is detached and you lie inside the boom with the mast base pointing forwards as you paddle the board. Useful for a broken UJ, but once again difficult in any breeze.

Additional Methods

Towing

The towed board should be positioned to windward. If the person being towed cannot hold onto the footstrap or the mast foot, use a piece of rope, harness, harness-line or even an uphaul to help them to hold onto the towing board.

Broken boom

If the side you need to get back to the shore is broken, reverse the boom to make a jury rig using the in and outhaul lines to secure. It might not feel great but it could get you ashore.

Broken Fin & Harness

Even with no fin you can sail by heavily tilting or digging the windward rail. Sheet in very gently and, whilst pulling the back of the board towards you with your back foot, try to avoid putting too much weight through the back foot. You come across the idea of removing your harness and securing it to the back of the board. However, this method is not as efficient as tilting the board, and almost impossible to do on modern wide-tailed boards!

Broken UJ

If a UJ breaks, tie the mast foot/extension to what is left of the UJ with spare cord or the downhaul line (taking care not to let-off the downhaul tension!). Ideally use a wetsuit boot or harness to protect the board.

Remember Windsurfing is a physical sport, so keep hydrated, especially in warmer climates.

Choosing a Windsurfing Location

Sailing at new and exciting locations, especially on the sea, is as much an important part of your windsurfing development as is venturing out in stronger winds, using larger rigs and travelling at faster speeds. The safety section and, above all, the Seven Common Senses (page 80, Safety and Self-rescue) should be read alongside the topics in this chapter to help you choose a suitable location from which to windsurf.

When choosing a location, you need to consider the following areas:

- Wind and weather conditions
- Local hazards – shallow areas, rocks, buoyage
- Getting on and off the water
- Tidal movements
- Other water users including shipping

Wind and Weather

Understanding a Weather Forecast

In the UK much of our weather is determined by Atlantic depressions.

On a weather map the depressions are shown by isobars that are lines of equal atmospheric pressure which are used to identify weather systems. They are used in a similar way to contours on a map.

There are two types of weather systems:

Low Pressure – Isobars tend to be closer together with the air moving in an anti-clockwise and inwards direction. The resulting conditions tend to be warm, wet and windy – exciting times for most windsurfers.

High Pressure – Isobars tend to be further apart with the air flowing in a clockwise and outwards direction. The resulting conditions tend to be cool, calm and clear with lighter winds - frustrating times for most windsurfers! All may not be lost, however, as local effects can still create sea breezes. (see page 92).

Weather forecasts, appropriate for windsurfing, need to be studied to check the likelihood of wind, its strength and if it is blowing in the right direction for a specific location. This information is available through various sources – Internet, television, radio, phone, fax, newspapers, local windsurfing shops, or your local RYA Training Centre.

Wind strength

Wind speed is measured in miles per hour or knots. 1 knot is equivalent to 1.1 miles per hour. The ideal wind strength for progressing towards planing and learning to use the harness and footstraps is between 7 – 21 knots or force 3 – 5 on the Beaufort Scale.

Wind Direction

There are two main ways of referring to wind direction:

1. Using the points of the compass – the wind direction describes where the wind is coming from. For example, a southerly wind is when the wind is blowing from the south.

2. Relative to the shoreline – wind direction can be described as onshore, cross-shore or offshore. Combinations of these terms are also used eg: cross-onshore.

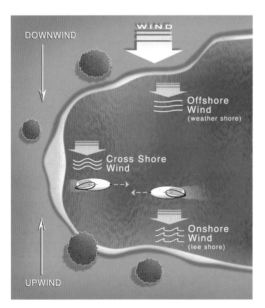

Cross-onshore or cross-shore winds are generally favoured wind directions for windsurfers. Make sure that you take transits (see page 91) and look for a landing point directly downwind of where you are sailing in case you are unable to stay upwind!

As highlighted in the 'seven common senses' the one wind direction to avoid is offshore.

- You will have a long walk or swim home if you break your kit or are unable to stay upwind, you may even get washed right out to sea.
- The wind strength may seem light and the water may look calm next to the shore, but further out the wind will almost certainly be a lot stronger and the water will get progressively rougher – not good conditions for you to improve your windsurfing skills!

Tides

Whatever your level, as soon as you go windsurfing in the sea, you need knowledge of both general tidal effects and local tidal characteristics. An understanding of tides plays an essential role in making windsurfing safe and enjoyable.

Tidal Movement

There are two elements to tides both of which affect windsurfers - vertical and horizontal movements.

Vertical Movement

The movement of water up and down a beach or sea wall, known as tidal range. Vertical movement varies daily and from area to area.

When the water is rising, the tide is coming in or flooding.

When the water is falling, the tide is going out or ebbing.

The difference between high and low water is approximately 6 hours. The rate of flow between high and low water can be generalized by the 'Rule of Twelfths'. The diagram below illustrates how much water flows during a given hour.

The diagram shows that the greatest movement of water is during the middle two hours and the least, either side of low and high water.

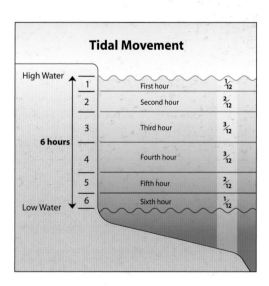

- If we take the two middle hours - 3rd and 4th hour, we can see 6/12 or ½ of the water will flow during this time. This shows that during this time frame we experience the fastest tidal flow.

- During hours 1 and 6, you will notice that only 1/12th of the water will flow during each of these times, therefore the slowest tidal movement during the 6 hour period.

March			March		
21	0031	5.0	**25**	0318	4.3
	0602	0.3		0857	1.3
	1250	4.9		1556	4.1
	1823	0.3		2127	1.6
22	0112	4.9	**26**	0412	3.9
	0643	0.4		1005	1.7
	1333	4.8		1705	3.8
	1904	0.5		2249	2.0
23	0153	4.8	**27**	0531	3.6
	0724	0.6		1139	1.9
	1417	4.6		1848	3.7
	1945	0.8			
24	0243	4.6	**28**	0029	2.1
	0807	0.9		0723	3.6
	1503	4.4		1313	1.8
	2030	1.2		2016	3.9

Dates in red are springs Dates in blue are neaps

This is a Tide Timetable

You can find out what the vertical tides are doing and how they will affect your local coastal venue by using tide timetables (tide-tables), available from local newsagents and harbour offices.

In some extreme locations a strongly ebbing tide could pull a windsurfer out to sea, but at most coastal locations – such tidal movements simply mean that the sea level rises and falls. When it does fall there may not be enough water left for you to continue windsurfing!

Horizontal Movement

This effect of the tide flooding or ebbing is moving along parallel to the coastline usually called Tidal Stream. As we have seen though The Rule of Twelfths, the rate of water flow varies throughout the time period between High and Low water. More specific information about tidal streams is found in a tidal stream atlas.

When choosing a new sailing location on coastal waters knowledge of the rate and direction of the tidal stream is important as this can affect your position on the water. When out on the water transits can be taken which help you to visually check your position. The taking of transits can also help you to understand the strength of the tidal stream.

What causes tidal movement?

The gravitational pull of the Moon, the Sun and the rotation of the Earth. This gives two periods of high and two of low water each 24 hour period.

There are approximately twelve hours between each high water and six hours between and high and low water.

- There are actually 24 hours and 50 minutes between daily tides, hence the reason for high and low water becoming later each day!

- Tides are also affected by monthly variations, due to changes in the strength in the gravitational pull. These differences are known as Springs and Neaps.

Spring and Neap tides

The amount of tidal rise and fall is dependent on the time of month. Every two weeks at a full and a new Moon, the Sun and Moon are aligned and therefore boost the gravitational pull. This produces the largest tidal range (a spring tide) and, therefore, the greatest movement of water, resulting in higher high tides and lower low tides. A smaller tidal range can be seen between a New and Full Moon – a neap tide, which are lower high tides and higher low tides.

This is explained easiest by looking at a tide timetable where you will see the difference each day in tidal heights over a two week period (see page 88).

Wind and Tide Awareness

Wind Strength – Spotting gusts and lulls

It is vital when windsurfing to be constantly aware of variations in the wind.

- Gusts – increase in wind speed
- Lulls – decrease in wind speed

As you sail along you can look over your leading shoulder and spot the following effects.

Differing strengths of wind make fish scales or dark patches (ripples) on the surface. Smooth or calmer water generally indicates less wind speed, a temporary lull. As the wind freshens, or during a gust, the density of such effects increases, causing the water to become disturbed or choppy, possibly leading to the formation of small waves.

If you sail within 4-5 mast lengths behind or downwind of another windsurfer, you will be affected by the water state and wind turbulence from their board and rig.

Gauging the wind strength in order to select an appropriate sail size is a skill that you'll gradually develop. Hand held wind speed readers (anemometers) can be useful as a guide to wind strength but one of the best ways of working out what to rig up is to ask other windsurfers preferably of a similar weight and ability as yourself what size kit they are using. Do not be afraid to approach other windsurfers for their advice on kit and conditions, this is common practice on windsurfing shores and is a great way to get to know the locals.

What's under the water?

The gradient of the beach will determine what the sea state is at different tide levels. This is why it is always a good idea to have a look at a new location at different states of tide and ask others for advice so you can gain more knowledge.

Depth of the water

Tides flow faster in deeper channels than in shallow water. For example in an estuary, where the water is likely to be deeper in the middle, the tidal flow will be greater in the middle than it will be by the shore.

Land mass

An increase of water flow occurs when tidal streams meet and/or are disrupted by an island, headland or submerged object. This can lead to unusual tidal patterns and water states and may make your windsurfing unnecessarily challenging. Again, local knowledge can help you identify where such hazards are and how best to deal with them or avoid them altogether.

Tidal Movements

Wind against tide

Wind blowing against tidal flow can produce choppy or even very rough conditions especially if the tidal flow is strong. This may be ideal for the experts looking for a bit of 'air time', not so good for the intermediate looking for a smooth stable ride! For further information on tide and tidal movement see tides page 87.

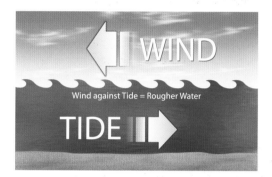

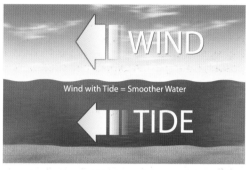

Wind against tide can also act as an upwind escalator

The tide will take you towards the wind, effectively increasing the wind speed. Especially useful on marginal days, where there may be only just enough wind to get you planing, allowing you to practise your technique safe in the knowledge that you are not going to end up miles downwind!

Wind with tide

Wind blowing with the tide effectively decreases the wind speed. It also produces flatter water but with the added risk that you do have to keep sailing upwind to maintain your position. Rigging a bigger sail than you would normally use on a non-tidal or wind against tide venue will help you stay upwind.

Transits

A simple transit is a line between your position on the water and a static visual reference point on the water (moored boats or buoys) or ashore (building). If the landscape behind this line appears to be stationary then you are not being affected by the tidal stream. If the landscape appears to be moving to the right or the left of the transit, then you are being moved along by the tide, possibly away from your original launching position and sailing line across the wind.

If you choose to sail when the wind and tide are flowing in the same direction, keeping a transit is essential to ensure that you are not drifting too far downwind and down tide. Using the place from where you launched can be the perfect transit and goal point, so remember to glance back several times as you sail away from the shore and take note of what your launch site looks like from the water.

Local Weather and its Effects

Wind often differs from what has been forecast which can be very frustrating to the windsurfer. Two windsurfers discussing their day on the water, may find that they have had very different experiences even though they were sailing only a few miles away from each other.

Such differences can be due to the geography of the land especially on large waters surrounded by hills producing its own localised climatic effects. In some wind directions this can produce funneling (venturi effects). For example, a prevailing Force 2 wind squeezed between two hills can exit the end of the valley at twice the strength. This kind of knowledge can usually only be gained from local windsurfers. As you start to windsurf regularly at alternative locations, in different conditions, you will soon pick up on the local knowledge and become a better informed and competent windsurfer.

There are other local effects that can cause the weather to vary from the forecast. For example on bright summer days when the wind is light in the morning, there's a good chance of a sea-breeze later on in the day.

Sea-breeze – thermal wind generated by the temperature difference between the land and the sea.

As the land warms up throughout the day warm air rises up off the land. This air is replaced by cooler air drawn off the sea which may generate a brisk on-wind, either in the same direction, or a different direction, to that forecast. This effect tends to peak by mid-afternoon and can reach a good Force 4.

The presence of strong sunshine is not a guarantee of a sea-breeze as even a light local wind can sometimes destroy this effect. A tell-tale sign that a sea-breeze is on its way, is the formation of light, fluffy clouds over the coast. A sign of hot air rising and condensing.

For more in-depth knowledge on weather patterns check out the RYA Weather Handbook (G1 www.rya.org.uk)

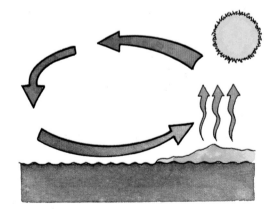

Rights of Way

Avoid collisions at all costs

As a golden rule, you should always avoid collisions, most can be avoided if you are watchful and considerate to other water users.

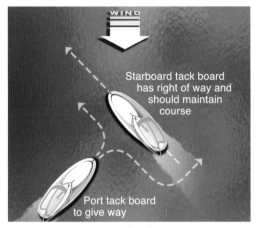

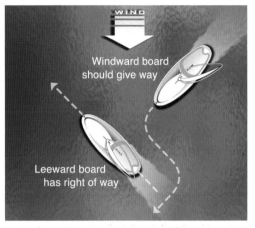

Port gives way to Starboard

If you are sailing on port tack you should keep out of the way of another board or sailing boat that is sailing in the opposite direction on starboard tack.

Windward gives way to Leeward

When two boards are sailing on the same tack, the windward board (the one closest to the source of the wind) must give way to the leeward board.

Overtaking

When a board or sailing boat is passing another board or sailing boat, the overtaking vessel must keep clear. In addition, and to avoid confusion, the vessel ahead must hold its course to allow the overtaking vessel to pass either side.

Other Craft

As a general guideline, a power vessel (a boat with an engine) should normally give way to a sailing vessel (windsurfer, dinghy, yacht). However, as a manoeuvreable craft, a windsurfer must stay well clear of any vessel that is restricted in its ability to manoeuvre eg. ferries, fishing trawlers in operation and supertankers. In general it is advisable to stay out of all shipping channels.

> **Top Tip**
> - If your right hand is forward on the boom, this means you're on starboard tack and most of the time have right of way.

So What's Next?

Now that you have been introduced to and hopefully developed many of the key skills involved in windsurfing, you are on the road to an exciting and rewarding future in the sport. While people participate at whatever pace suits them, there is a great army of windsurfers throughout the world who have enjoyed taking their windsurfing on to a higher level.

Progression towards the more advanced levels of windsurfing is both enjoyable and rewarding. Success is down to the amount of time on the water, good coaching and always focusing on the techniques covered in this book. In time you will be able to really enjoy all the benefits of the sport including whizzing around in new and thrilling locations.

Advanced course

As you grow in confidence you will be seeking out stronger winds in order to blast about on your local stretch of water.

Waterstarts are a key skill in the Advanced Course and, once you have mastered harness, footstraps and waterstarts, you can venture onto lower volume boards. These boards are easier to manoeuvre in stronger winds and are great fun.

A perfect planing gybe is one of the most sought-after and stimulating aspects of advanced windsurfing. Carving a fast arc can test you to your limits and the reward for sailing out of it with real speed is a feeling that is indescribable!

A Windsurfer's Glossary – part 1

Apparent wind — Combination of true wind and induced wind.

Battens — Stiff, flexible rods providing strength and shape to sail.

Beam reach — Direction approximately 90° away from direction of the wind.

Blasting — Moving quickly across the water.

Blasting control — Control of the board and rig when moving quickly across the water

Boom — The 'handlebars' of a windsurfer

Broad reach — Direction approximately 135° away from direction of wind.

Buoyancy aid — Foam-filled jacket providing positive buoyancy when immersed

Butterfly rescue — Self-rescue where sail is laid on the board and sailor paddles.

Catapulted — Being propelled forwards off the board by the sail.

Centreline — Imaginary line along the centre of the board from nose to tail

Clew — Rear (lower) corner of sail, which attaches to the end of the boom

Daggerboard — Large flat retractable plate providing board with sideways resistance

Deck plate — Fitting in board into which mastfoot is secured.

Downhaul — Rope used to attach tack of sail to mastfoot, enabling rig tuning

Fastfwd Formula — Coaching model used within the National Windsurfing Scheme:

    Vision: Looking where you want to go.

    Trim: Ensuring board is kept flat.

    Counterbalance: Balancing the body's weight against the power of the sail

    Power: Sheeting the boom in.

    Stance: Body position while sailing

Fin — Curved foil attached to underside and tail of board providing directional stability.

Flagging — Downwind self-rescue

'Gear gazing' — Looking at rig too much instead of where you are going.

Gybing — Turn taking the nose of the board away from the wind.

Harness — Equipment to attach the body to the rig.

Harness lines — Lines linking harness to rig.

Hooking in — Attaching harness to harness lines.

IMCS — Indexed Mast Curve System – international standard for measuring stiffness of mast.

Induced wind — Wind created by forward movement of board.

Isobars — Lines of equal atmospheric pressure on weather maps.

Jury rig — Temporary repair to rig enabling self-rescue.

Laminar flow — Smooth airflow across sail providing lift.

Leech — Trailing edge of sail

Leeward — Side of the board away from the wind

Lift — Force acting on sail to power the board forward.

A Windsurfer's Glossary – part 2

Luff tube — Tube in leading edge of sail into which mast is fitted.

Luffing — Altering course towards wind.

Mast extension — Adjustable version of a mastfoot.

Mastfoot — Attachment joining board and rig together.

Neap tide — Smaller tide range caused by phase of Moon.

Nose — Front of the board.

'Nose over Toes' — Stance keeping head above feet.

npcg — Non-planing carve gybe

Outhaul — Rope used to attach clew of the sail to end of boom.

Planing — Where board reaches sufficient speed to travel on the minimal of wetted area on the surface of water

Rail — Edge of board

Rash vest — T-shirt like garment worn to provide protection.

Rig Rotator — Specific movement of the rig in gybes.

Rotational sails — Sails where battens provide aerofoil shape by being set (rotating) around mast.

Sail quiver — Set of different-sized sails

Sea-breeze — Thermal wind generated by temperature difference between land and sea

Sheeting in — Pulling the boom in, back and down.

Shifting & Switching — Specific footwork movement during a transition

Spinning out — Board slides sideways after loss of grip.

Spring tide — Larger tide range caused by phase of Moon.

Tacking — Turn taking the nose of the board through the wind.

Tail — Back of the board

Tidal range — Vertical movement of water

Tidal stream — Movement of water parallel to coastline

Transit — Position judged by lining up two objects.

Transitions — Tacking and gybing

True wind — Prevailing wind when standing still

Tuning — Adjustment of rig to find most efficient set-up.

Turbulent flow — Disturbed airflow over sail

Turtle rescue — Self-rescue where sail is laid on board and sailor paddles with sail above

Twin-cam sails — Sails with larger luff tubes accommodating device to hold the batten against the mast

UJ (universal joint) — Part of mastfoot, allowing flexible movement of the rig

Uphaul — Combined rope and elastic attached to boom enabling rig to be pulled out of the water

Wetsuit — Neoprene suit to keep the body protected and warm.

Windward — Side of the board closer to the wind

Index

Index

RYA Windsurfing

Log your progression with the **National Windsurfing Scheme Logbook and Syllabus (G47)**

Designed as a logbook suitable for beginner, intermediate and advanced windsurfers, this book also contains essential information on the new and improved RYA Windsurfing Syllabus. It clearly explains how to choose the right course, outlines the content of the syllabus and states the assessment criteria that will be used. RYA National Windsurfing Scheme Logbook and Syllabus also includes a personal log, on which to chart progress, notes pages and space for readers to attach their certificates.

RYA Intermediate Windsurfing (G51)

RYA Intermediate Windsurfing builds on the manoeuvres learnt in Start Windsurfing. It covers the effective and memorable coaching system, how to get to grips with the harness and footstraps, beachstarting, equipment, and developing tacks and gybes ready for a little more wind.

Written by Simon Bornhoft and edited by Amanda Van Santen.

RYA Advanced Windsurfing (G52)

Blasting control, waterstarting, tacking, gybing, bump and jump, and advanced carving skills are developed from the intermediate course, continuing the use of coaching and enhancing theoretical knowledge. Each skill, transition or piece of information is explained step by step and combined with photographs or illustrations.

Written by Simon Bornhoft and edited by Amanda Van Santen.

The RYA provides courses encouraging and helping people to become qualified Instructors. Following the same levels as the National Scheme, each instructor course is taught by highly qualified and trained coaches at RYA Training Centres. If you want to pass on your skills and encourage others into the sport of windsurfing, course dates are available on the RYA website **www.rya.org.uk** or by calling RYA Training on **02380 604 181**. All pre and post instructor course information for all levels is also covered in the W33 Instructor Handbook.

All RYA publications are available online from the RYA Webshop www.rya.org.uk or via the RYA Despatch department on: 0845 345 0372

RYA Membership

Promoting and Protecting Boating

www.rya.org.uk

RYA Membership

Promoting and Protecting Boating

The RYA is the national organisation which represents the interests of everyone who goes boating for pleasure.

The greater the membership, the louder our voice when it comes to protecting members' interests.

Apply for membership today, and support the RYA, to help the RYA support you.

Benefits of Membership

- Access to expert advice on all aspects of boating from legal wrangles to training matters
- Special members' discounts on a range of products and services including boat insurance, books, videos and class certificates
- Free issue of certificates of competence, increasingly asked for by everyone from overseas governments to holiday companies, insurance underwriters to boat hirers

- Access to the wide range of RYA publications, including the quarterly magazine
- Third Party insurance for windsurfing members
- Free Internet access with RYA-Online
- Special discounts on AA membership
- Regular offers in RYA Magazine
- ...and much more

Join now - membership form opposite

Join online at www.rya.org.uk

Visit our website for information, advice, members' services and web shop.

1 Important To help us comply with Data Protection legislation, please tick *either* Box A or Box B (you must tick Box A to ensure you receive the full benefits of RYA membership). The RYA will not pass your data to third parties.

☐ **A.** I wish to join the RYA and receive future information on member services, benefits (as listed in RYA Magazine and website) and offers.

☐ **B.** I wish to join the RYA but do not wish to receive future information on member services, benefits (as listed in RYA Magazine and website) and offers.

When completed, please send this form to: RYA, RYA House, Ensign Way, Hamble, Southampton, SO31 4YA

2

Title	Forename	Surname	Date of Birth			Male	Female
			D D / M M / Y Y			☐	☐
1.							
2.			D D / M M / Y Y			☐	☐
3.			D D / M M / Y Y			☐	☐
4.			D D / M M / Y Y			☐	☐

Address

Town   County   Post Code

Evening Telephone   Daytime Telephone

email

Signature: _____   Date: _____

3 Type of membership required: *(Tick Box)*

☐ *Personal* Annual rate £39 or £36 by Direct Debit

☐ *Under 21* Annual rate £13 *(no reduction for Direct Debit)*

☐ *Family** Annual rate £58 or £55 by Direct Debit

* Family Membership: 2 adults plus any under 21s all living at the same address

4 Please tick ONE box to show your main boating interest.

☐ Yacht Racing   ☐ Yacht Cruising
☐ Dinghy Racing   ☐ Dinghy Cruising
☐ Personal Watercraft   ☐ Inland Waterways
☐ Powerboat Racing   ☐ Windsurfing
☐ Motor Boating   ☐ Sportsboats and RIBs

Please see Direct Debit form overleaf

![RYA logo]

Instructions to your Bank or Building Society to pay by Direct Debit

![Direct Debit logo]

Please complete this form and return it to:
Royal Yachting Association, RYA House, Ensign Way, Hamble, Southampton, Hampshire SO31 4YA

Originators Identification Number

9	5	5	2	1	3

5. RYA Membership Number (For office use only)

To The Manager: Bank/Building Society

Address:

Post Code:

2. Name(s) of account holder(s)

3. Branch Sort Code

	—		—	

4. Bank or Building Society account number

6. Instruction to pay your Bank or Building Society

Please pay Royal Yachting Association Direct Debits from the account detailed in this instruction subject to the safeguards assured by The Direct Debit Guarantee.
I understand that this instruction may remain with the Royal Yachting Association and, if so, details will be passed electronically to my Bank/Building Society.

Signature(s) _____

Date _____

Banks and Building Societies may not accept Direct Debit instructions for some types of account

Cash, Cheque, Postal Order enclosed £ _____
Made payable to the Royal Yachting Association

Office use only: Membership Number Allocated

Office use / Centre Stamp

077